I0259367

BE WORTHY OF PEACE

William E. Londèa

AIVEON ENTERPRISES

New York

© 2016 William E. Londèa
All rights reserved.

No part of this publication may be
reproduced, stored in a retrieval system or
transmitted in any form or by any means
electronic, mechanical, photocopying,
recording or otherwise without the prior
written permission of the publisher.

ISBN: 978-0-9890777-4-3

Published by Aiveon Enterprises
535 West 162nd Street, #34
New York, NY 10032

Printed in the United States of America

"forsan et haec olim meminisse iuvabi"

("Perhaps even these things will be good to remember one day.")

_Virgil, The Aeneid, Book 1

~ 1 ~

BEFORE PLAYING THE FOOL

REHEARSE

~ 2 ~

THE HUMBLE

HAVE LITTLE NEED OF A TRUMPET

~ 3 ~

CAT MOVES IN

MOUSE MOVES OUT

IT'S NOT INDULGENCE

WHEN DEEMED NECESSARY

~ 5 ~

DON'T JEOPARDIZE

COMPROMISE

~ 6 ~

CHILDREN ARE MESSAGES

SENT TO A FUTURE WE MAY NOT SEE

~ 7 ~

BECAUSE YOU CAN

DOESN'T MEAN YOU SHOULD

DON'T EXTEND EVIL AN INVITATION

AND PRESUME IT MIGHT DECLINE

~ 9 ~

ADVISE

ONLY WHEN ASKED

~ 10 ~

ONCE YOU BELIEVE

YOU'VE WON HALF THE STRUGGLE

~ 11 ~

ARROGANCE COSTS

~ 12 ~

CURRENT EVENT

HISTORIC ACCOUNT

~ 13 ~

WITH FREEDOM

COMES CONSEQUENCES

~ 14 ~

IF THERE WAS ONLY ONE WAY

VENUS WOULD BE AN ANOMALY

ACCOMMODATE AND TOLERATE

ARE NOT SYNONYMS

~ 16 ~

LIFE IS TOUGH

BE TOUGHER

~ 17 ~

LEAD, FOLLOW, GUIDE OR WATCH

BUT CHOOSE

~ 18 ~

DON'T TELL

SHOW

~ 19 ~

ASK TOO MANY QUESTIONS

GET TOO MANY ANSWERS

~ 20 ~

THINK NOT TOO LONG

THINK NOT TOO HARD

~ 21 ~

A HALF TRUTH

IS A WHOLE LIE

~ 22 ~

THERE ARE UNOPENED DOORS

THAT SHOULD REMAIN SO

~ 23 ~

AN ANSWER

MAY NOT BE THE ANSWER

~ 24 ~

INCESSANT WHINING

GIVES CAUSE TO YAWN

~ 25 ~

CAUSE OF THE BEGINNING

CAUSE OF THE END

~ 26 ~

DON'T RUE THE DAY

RULE THE DAY

~ 27 ~

LEARN NOW

UNDERSTAND LATER

~ 28 ~

LEARN THE RULES

THEN PLAY THE GAME

A BOAT WITH TOO LARGE A HOLE

CANNOT RISE WITH THE TIDE

~ 30~

HAPPINESS

WHEN "I" BECOMES "WE"

~ 31 ~

A LITTLE MAY EASE

A LOT MAY CURE

HATE JUDICIOUSLY

~ 33 ~

SMALL SPARK

BIG FIRE

TWO FEET

TWO SHOES

~ 35 ~

YOU MAY BATTLE ANOTHER

BUT YOU WAR WITH YOURSELF

THE TRUTH WILL SET YOU FREE

AND PROBABLY PISS YOU OFF

A GOOD TEST OF FRIENDSHIP

IS HOW YOU GREET EACH OTHER

AFTER LONG PERIODS OF ABSENCE

DON'T DO WRONG

THEN EXPECT THINGS TO GO RIGHT

~ 39 ~

PROCREATING

DOES NOT MAKE ONE A PARENT

~ 40 ~

LEARN FROM THE PAST

LIVE IN THE PRESENT

PREPARE FOR THE FUTURE

SAYING THANK YOU WILL SUFFICE

SAYING MORE CHANCES CONCEIT

~ 42 ~

SOME ENEMIES

SUPPOSE THEMSELVES FRIENDS

~ 43 ~

A STARVED DOG

WILL EAT ITS MASTER

~ 44 ~

PLENTY HEAR

NOT ENOUGH LISTEN

~ 45 ~

THE UNIVERSE

RECYCLES EVERYTHING

FISH MAY BE SLIPPERY

BUT THEY STILL GET CAUGHT

IN OUR KEEP

NOT OURS TO KEEP

~ 48 ~

ASSESS THEN COMMENCE

~ 49 ~

RIGHT STONE REMOVED

STRONGEST WALL COLLAPSES

~ 50 ~

FORGET THE DISTRACTION

REMEMBER THE GOAL

~ 51 ~

A ROLL OF DICE

AND ALL IS LOST

~ 52 ~

BE ASSURED AS MUCH AS POSSIBLE

BEFORE

TO FATHOM THE NEED FOR ORDER

WITNESS DISORDER

PARENTS ARE NOT THE SOURCE

MERELY THE CONDUIT

THE NATURE OF THE BEAST

YESTERDAY, TODAY, ALWAYS

~ 56 ~

FAME

PAYS NEITHER RENT NOR TAXES

RIGHT RESPONSE

TRUMPS FAST RESPONSE

~ 58 ~

SEE THE WIN

IN AN HONEST DEFEAT

~ 59 ~

LOVE BESTOWED

IS AS THE DAY SPENT

~ 60 ~

AS THERE ARE SECRETS

THERE ARE WARRANTS

CLARITY CAN BE FLEETING

~ 62 ~

SILENCE

MAY BE THE WISER RESPONSE

ANGELS GET THEIR WINGS FROM GOD

HUMANS GET THEIRS FROM FEAR

IT'S A BIG WORLD

UNTIL YOU RUN INTO SOMEONE

YOU HOPED YOU'D NEVER SEE AGAIN

ALCOHOL DOES NOT POUR ITSELF

~ 66 ~

NOT NOW

RIGHT NOW

DIFFICULT

YES

IMPOSSIBLE

NO

~ 68 ~

COULD HAVE BUT DIDN'T

SAVES AND CONDEMNS

BEFORE YOU ASK THE QUESTION

BE SATISFIED

IT'S THE ONE YOU WANT TO ASK

~ 70 ~

LIVING IN SHADOW

IS A DEATH UNTO ITSELF

BY WAY OF DENIAL

DO MANY SEE ANOTHER DAY

DINOSAURS ARE NOT EXTINCT

THEY'RE SMART

~ 73 ~

CHOOSE YOUR LIES

CAREFULLY

~ 74 ~

TOUCH YOURSELF

YOU WON'T BITE

WHAT CHILDREN ARE

ADULTS CAN ONLY MIMIC

~ 76 ~

IN LARGE AND SMALL MEASURES

WE ALL FALTER

BEING SMART

IS NOT THE SAME AS

BEING INTELLIGENT

DON'T FIGHT

A FIRE BREATHING DRAGON

WITH A WOODEN SWORD

LIFE IS A STRONG ARGUMENT

IN FAVOR OF REINCARNATION

AN ANGRY CHILD

IS ONE THING

AN ANGRY ADULT

BEHAVING LIKE AN ANGRY CHILD

IS QUITE ANOTHER

~ 81 ~

YOU CAN'T SEE YOUR REFLECTION

FROM INSIDE A MIRROR

IF HELPING IS NOT YOUR INTENT

MIND YOUR BUSINESS

A FRIEND TO EVERYONE

IS A FRIEND TO NO ONE

~ 84 ~

IN THE MIDST OF DARKNESS

REMEMBER THERE IS ALSO LIGHT

~ 85 ~

THERE'S NOTHING WRONG

WITH BEING YOUR OWN FAN CLUB

~ 86 ~

FROM A TRICKLE

COMES A FLOOD

~ 87 ~

ONE PLANET

MANY WORLDS

HASTY PRAISE

SNAKE IN THE GRASS

SOME THINGS SHOULD ONLY BE DONE

IN THE PRIVACY OF YOUR MIND

GOD DISAPPOINTS

BUT NEVER FAILS

TOLD ONE

TOLD ALL

BE SUCCESSFUL

IN SPITE OF YOURSELF

WHAT YOU NEED

IS PROVIDED

WHAT YOU WANT

YOU MUST ASK FOR

OR

PROVIDE YOURSELF

~ 94 ~

THE FIRST BETRAYAL

COMES FROM WITHIN

MANY ARE QUICK TO JUDGE

FEW ARE QUICK TO COUNSEL

~ 96 ~

YOU'RE RIGHT

ONLY UNTIL YOU'RE WRONG

TOWARDS ONE

AWAY FROM ANOTHER

~ 98 ~

WHEN READY TO STAND OUT

STAND UP

FAILURE IS A CHOICE

AS MUCH AS IT IS A RESULT

~ 100 ~

THOSE WHO DO GOOD

CAN ALSO DO BAD

FEEL HAPPINESS

EXPERIENCE JOY

~ 102 ~

IF IT ISN'T BROKEN

YOU CAN'T FIX IT

~ 103 ~

I LOVE YOU

DOESN'T MEAN I TRUST YOU

ABSENT KNOWING

ALLY CAUTION

BELIEVE YOU WILL FAIL

AND YOU PROBABLY WILL

ONLY A FOOL

LISTENS TO ONE

~ 107 ~

PRAY AS YOU GO

~ 108 ~

PROFIT

FROM WHAT OTHERS SQUANDER

~ 109 ~

MANNERS

DON'T LEAVE HOME WITHOUT THEM

PERCEPTION IS SO

TO THE WILLFULLY BLIND

~ 111 ~

GET UP AND GO

BEFORE YOUR GET UP AND GO

GETS UP AND GOES WITHOUT YOU

~ 112~

SALVATION

IS NOT A GIVEN

~ 113~

HOW YOU USE YOUR MIND

IS UP TO YOU

CHILDREN ARE INQUISITIVE

EVERYONE ELSE IS NOSY

~ 115~

THE MAJORITY

HAS BEEN WRONG BEFORE

~ 116~

MONEY

MATTERS

BETTER BY CHOICE

THAN BY FIAT

~ 118 ~

DON'T BLAME GOD

FOR YOUR BAD DECISIONS

ENRICH NEED

BESMIRCH GREED

MANY CAN PLAY THE NOTES

FEW CAN PLAY THE MUSIC

EVIDENCE IS JUST THAT

~ 122 ~

SEEK THE WORST

FIND THE WORST

ALL ROADS END

~ 124 ~

THE SERPENT NEED NOT BE REMINDED

TO SHED WORN SKIN

DON'T EQUATE THE LESSON

WITH THE TEACHER

IT'S NOT TRUTH THAT HURTS

IT'S UNTRUTH...RESISTING EXPULSION

KNOW LITTLE

LEARN MUCH

~ 128 ~

IN THE PURSE

TILL TIME TO DISPERSE

TAKE ONE

GIVE TWO

~ 130 ~

DON'T TRY TO BUY

WHAT CAN ONLY BE RENTED

~ 131 ~

WOMAN LED

MAN FOLLOWED

IF PRAYER HARMS ONLY YOUR PRIDE

COUNT YOUR BLESSINGS

TRULY GIVE

IT'S NOT THE DEAL

IT'S THE PLAY

THEY THAT MASTER

TOO MUST SERVE

BITING YOUR TONGUE

MAY SAVE YOUR TEETH

OPTIMISTS

CHALLENGE MACHINES

~ 138 ~

TROUBLE ANOTHER'S HOME

TROUBLE YOUR OWN

SEEDS OF ENVY

GROW SOUR GRAPES

~ 140 ~

SOME KNOW A LITTLE ABOUT A LOT

SOME KNOW A LOT ABOUT NOTHING

LIVE IT OUT

BETTER TO LIVE

AND BE ANGRY WITH GOD

THAN TO DIE

AND GOD BE ANGRY WITH YOU

DON'T FREAK OUT

REACH OUT

~ 144 ~

IF YOU HAD ALL THE ANSWERS

YOUR PRESENCE

WOULD BE UNNECESSARY

DENY THYSELF AND RECEIVE

~ 146 ~

LET PRIDE

BE A SUBJECT OF CONFIDENCE

THE DAY WILL NOT GO FASTER

BECAUSE YOU'RE IN A HURRY

DON'T LET A BAD PAST

STIFLE A PROMISING FUTURE

HYPOCRISY

IS SELDOM POORLY DRESSED

DON'T CHAMPION WHAT YOU BELIEVE

FOR WHAT YOU KNOW

DON'T REGRET THE PAST

LEARN FROM IT

~ 152 ~

EVEN IF YOU'VE WALKED

IN ANOTHER'S SHOES

IT'S BEST NOT TO TELL THEM HOW TO

SO ALLOWED

SO REASONED

~ 154 ~

IF UNABLE TO REMAIN AS LOVERS

BETTER TO PART AS FRIENDS

WAR

IS THE OFFSPRING OF FEAR

THE DEAD DO NOT SPEAK

YET WE OFTEN HEAR FROM THEM

REPETITION MULLED

APOLOGY NULLED

~ 158 ~

APPRECIATE

THE VALUE OF TIME

EVIL

IS AN EQUAL OPPORTUNIST

EVEN THAT WHICH TAKES FLIGHT

MUST EVENTUALLY SET DOWN

TO BETTER COMPREHEND

SIMPLIFY

BIG FLAME

SMALL FLAME

BOTH BURN

JUST THE SAME

ENGAGE YOUR MIND

BEFORE YOU ENGAGE YOUR MOUTH

~ 164 ~

SOME PEOPLE WILL NEVER CHANGE

PERHAPS YOU SHOULD

WITHOUT HOUSE RULES

THERE IS NO HOUSE

WHAT YOU ARE

IS NOT NECESSARILY

WHO YOU ARE

THERE'S NO REMEMBERING

WHAT NEVER HAPPENED

~ 168 ~

DON'T LET YOUR EXPRESSIONS

BETRAY YOUR THOUGHTS

USE REJECTION

AS YOU WOULD A STEPPINGSTONE

~ 170 ~

FEW ARE INTERESTED

IN WHAT YOU USED TO

~ 171 ~

NATURE

LETS US BELIEVE WE'VE WON

~ 172 ~

OURS TO USE

NOT OURS TO ABUSE

ERRING IS INEVITABLE

FORGIVE YOURSELF

YOU CAN TALK ABOUT

OR

YOU CAN BE ABOUT

~ 175 ~

WISDOM GRANTED

BEST NOT IGNORED

BETTER FALSE TEETH

THAN FALSE FRIENDS

TIME ADVANCES

POTENTIAL RETREATS

~ 178 ~

DON'T WORRY

WHEN PEOPLE TALK ABOUT YOU

WORRY

WHEN THEY STOP

FOR CLUES TO A HAPPY LIFE

LOOK TO A HAPPY CHILD

TODAY'S PROCRASTINATION

BECOMES TOMORROW'S CHORE

MORE THAN SOME

LESS THAN OTHERS

IF YOU DON'T BORROW

YOU DON'T OWE

LETTING OTHERS DOWN

DOESN'T MEAN YOU'VE FAILED THEM

VENTURE

BEYOND THE TIP OF YOUR NOSE

COMES ACCEPTANCE

COMES PEACE

THE CONCEPT

MIGHT WELL ECLIPSE

THE EXECUTION

IF IT'S NOT WORTH DISCUSSING

IT'S NOT WORTH ARGUING ABOUT

WHEN GIVING A PIECE OF YOUR MIND

BE SURE IT'S NOT A PIECE YOU NEED

TO KEEP FOR YOURSELF

~ 189 ~

SEE OTHERS FOR WHO THEY ARE

NOT FOR WHO YOU WISH THEM TO BE

IT'S NOT THE CONQUEST

IT'S THE PURSUIT

~ 191 ~

RETURN BLAME

TO ITS RIGHTFUL OWNER

IT'S ONLY MONEY

UNTIL YOU HAVEN'T ANY

~ 193 ~

AIM HATE WHERE YOU WILL

YOU STILL REMAIN ITS TARGET

AS THE BLOOM

SO THE CHARM

FAULT OR VIRTUE

WE REMEMBER

FOOL'S GOLD

FOOL'S FORTUNE

~ 197 ~

THERE ARE NO GOOD OR BAD DAYS

THERE ARE ONLY DAYS

WHEN GOOD OR BAD THINGS HAPPEN

~ 198 ~

BIG BROTHER

WATCHING BIG SISTER

WATCHING BIG BROTHER

~ 199 ~

THE EXPLANATION

MAY AMPLIFY THE MISDEED

~ 200 ~

ONE REASON TO LOVE

CAN VOID A THOUSAND REASONS

NOT TO

~ 201 ~

BEING BORN WITHOUT

WAS NOT YOUR DOING

REMAINING WITHOUT

COULD BE

IMAGINATION AND VARIATION

CONSULT

~ 203 ~

PRY

AND YOU MAY LIVE TO REGRET IT

~ 204 ~

IT'S NOT THE EARTH

THAT NEEDS SAVING

DON'T MAKE WAVES

UNLESS

YOU MEAN TO ROCK THE BOAT

SOMETIMES

THE LESS YOU SAY

THE MORE YOU'RE HEARD

TRUST BE DAMNED

TAKE THE LEAP

MASTER SMALL THINGS

THEY ARE PREPARATION

FOR BIG THINGS TO COME

~ 209 ~

REMEMBER

TODAY WAS ONCE TOMORROW

LOVE

EASIER TO DESCRIBE THAN DEFINE

~ 211 ~

THERE IS NO VALIDATION

FOR CRUELTY

MANY FAIL TO REALIZE

THE HOLE THEY'VE DUG

IS FOR THEMSELVES

UNTIL THEY'RE LOOKING UP

FROM DOWN INSIDE OF IT

TO FIND THE POT OF GOLD

AT THE END OF THE RAINBOW

ONE MUST FIRST FIND

THE END OF THE RAINBOW

DON'T DEBASE YOURSELF

ACE YOURSELF

HATE

CANNOT BECOME BENEVOLENCE

BUT IT CAN BE REPLACED BY IT

MANY HAVE FORGOTTEN

MORE THAN

MANY HAVE EVER LEARNED

~ 217 ~

IF YOU CAN'T LET GO OF YOUR PAST

AT LEAST BE AT PEACE WITH IT

THERE IS NO SEAT FOR VANITY

AT THE TABLE OF PERFECTION

IF YOU TAKE A SHORTCUT

EXPECT TO BE CUT SHORT

THE STAIRCASE FROM THE TOP

ONLY LEADS DOWN

NEITHER FAIR NOR UNFAIR

LIFE SIMPLY IS

STRIPING A LION

WON'T MAKE IT A TIGER

THERE ARE THOSE

WHO ARE IN NEED

AND THERE ARE THOSE

WHO ARE JUST LAZY

WHAT DWELLS INSIDE IS REVEALED

BY WHAT COMES OUT OF THE MOUTH

DON'T GAMBLE

WITH ANOTHER PERSON'S LIFE

GAMBLE ON LIFE

WITH ANOTHER PERSON

~ 226 ~

IT IS IMAGINABLE

BUT NOT POSSIBLE

TO SEE THROUGH ANOTHER'S EYES

THE ODDS WERE AGAINST CLEOPATRA

AND STILL SHE BECAME QUEEN

~ 228 ~

YOU ALREADY HAVE A SHADOW

YOU CAN WIN WITH LIFE

YOU CANNOT WIN AGAINST IT

BEING EMPOWERED

YIELDS BETTER RESULTS

THAN BEING EMBITTERED

NEVER FORGO AN OPPORTUNITY

TO BE A FRIEND

LIVE A LIFE

NOT A LIE

NOISE TO ONE

MUSIC TO ANOTHER

IT IS NOT WHO'S HATING WHOM

IT'S HATING

YOU CAN NEVER BE SOMEONE

OTHER THAN YOURSELF

~ 236 ~

NO WATER IN THE WELL

NO WATER IN THE BUCKET

IF YOU'VE NEVER SEEN EVIL

FACE TO FACE

PRAY YOU NEVER DO

~ 238 ~

NO MORTAL EYES

HAVE EVER SEEN AIR

IF BY CHANCE

YOU CATCH THE DEVIL SLEEPING

LEAVE IT BE

~ 240 ~

OPEN A MIND

CLOSE A PRISON

~ 241 ~

THERE'S NOTHING PRODUCTIVE

GOING ON UNDER YOUR BEHIND

GOD DOES NOT LIE

PEOPLE DO

ARMAMENTS DO NOT BRING PEACE

ONLY SUBMISSION

THERE ARE LAWS

AND THEN

THERE ARE THE LAWS

DON'T YEARN

FOR WHAT'S COME AND GONE

YOU CAN'T FOOL YOURSELF

BUT

YOU CAN MAKE A FOOL OF YOURSELF

HUNGER FOR JUSTICE

NOT REVENGE

~ 248 ~

THE ENEMY WITHIN

ENABLES THE ENEMY WITHOUT

~ 249 ~

HELPING OTHERS

HELPS YOU

~ 250 ~

ALL ARE GIVEN A SEASON

NOTHING FOR THE MASTER

NOTHING FOR THE SERVANT

NO ELDERS

NO YOUNGERS

TIME MATTERS MOST

TO THOSE WHO UNDERSTAND IT LEAST

DISBELIEF DOES NOT ELIMINATE FACT

~ 255 ~

COVETING A LIFE

OTHER THAN YOUR OWN

IS JUST...

DUMB

~ 256 ~

WHEN YOU TAKE FOR YOURSELF

YOU TAKE FROM SOMEONE ELSE

THOUGH YOU ACCOMPLISH

YOU ARE HELPED

A HELPING HAND

IS NOT A HANDOUT

LUCKY

BLESSED

EITHER

OR

~ 260 ~

DO WELL

DO GOOD

~ 261 ~

YOU CAN'T GIVE TO ANOTHER

WHAT ISN'T YOURS TO BEGIN WITH

WAYLAID PLANS

DO NOT JUSTIFY GIVING UP

WHEN EVERYONE IS IN THE WATER

IT IS DIFFICULT TO SPOT

THE ONE WHO IS DROWNING

LIFE DOES NOT ADHERE

TO YOUR AGENDA

BE FLEXIBLE

~ 265 ~

LIKE FOR LIKE

THE CREATED DOES NOT WITNESS

ITS OWN CREATION

YOU HAVE A JOB

GET TO IT

THINK

ABOUT SOMETHING ELSE

BE CANDID

NOT INSULTING

~ 270 ~

LIE

ONLY UPON DEMAND

~ 271 ~

NINE BROKE FRIENDS

CAN EASILY BECOME TEN

HERE BEFORE YOU

MORE THAN LIKELY

HERE AFTER YOU

DO NOT ASK A QUESTION

KNOWING ANOTHER CANNOT ANSWER

~ 274 ~

MASTER THYSELF

GOD DOES NOT SEND

WHAT YOU'RE NOT MEANT TO HAVE

~ 276 ~

RESPECT WHAT YOU DON'T KNOW

FROM SELF LOATHING TO SELF PITY

IS NOT PROGRESS

~ 278 ~

BURNED BRIDGES

CANNOT AGAIN BE CROSSED

THE HEART

TAKES NO PART IN DECEPTION

~ 280 ~

MANIFEST THE DREAM

LIFE'S PACE IS SET

SET YOURS

~ 282 ~

IF YOU CAN'T BE HONEST

BE SILENT

~ 283 ~

STATUS

DOES NOT DETERMINE

REGARD

DONT BE ANXIOUS FOR LETDOWNS

THEY WILL COME

BE WISE

TO THE EXTENT

OF YOUR INDEPENDENCE

LET COMPASSION BE CONTAGIOUS

THE PAST PRECEDES THE FUTURE

IT DOES NOT DICTATE

HISTORY IS ACCURATE

TO THOSE WHO RECORD IT

LOVING IS NORMAL

DEATH

CAN ONLY BE FOUGHT FOR SPORT

NOT VICTORY

DUPLICITY HINDERS EVOLUTION

OF FLESH AND BONE

PRIDE HAS NO STEWARD

GET BUSY

THOSE TO THE MANOR BORN

ARE NOT SPARED TRIBULATIONS

MAKE THE POINT OF NO RETURN

THE POINT OF A NEW BEGINNING

~ 296 ~

IF UNABLE TO DO FOR SELF

DO FOR OTHERS

EMBRACE THE POSSIBILITY

OF IMPROVING

ENGAGE ADVERSITY

ON AN AS NEEDED BASIS

SURELY SPRING WILL COME

~ 300 ~

DON'T LECTURE

WHEN YOU SHOULD LISTEN

THE EYE OF THE HURRICANE

IS OF NO COMFORT FROM THE WALL

IMAGINATION

SPAWNS OTHER THAN FEAR

THE AUDIENCE MAY BE DIFFERENT

BUT THE PLAY IS THE SAME

~ 304 ~

BE BETTER AT LEADING

THAN FOLLOWING

~ 305 ~

BEGIN

AGAIN

IF IT'S YOUR BAGGAGE

EVENTUALLY YOU MUST CARRY IT

REASON WHY

A THING CANNOT BE DONE

RID YOURSELF

OF INFERIOR ARMOR

~ 309 ~

DON'T LAMENT

WHO YOU ARE NOT

CELEBRATE

WHO YOU ARE

MONEY HAS NO FRIENDS

~ 311 ~

CONQUER ALL

ONE AT A TIME

~ 312 ~

CHILDREN GIVE REASONS

ADULTS GIVE EXCUSES

~ 313 ~

BAD BEGETS WORSE

WORSE BEGETS WORST

~ 314 ~

A HALF FILLED GLASS

IS NOT NECESSARILY A BAD THING

~ 315 ~

NO TEARS FROM DRY DUCTS

BETRAYAL RANGES FAR AND WIDE

~ 317 ~

BEING UNCONVENTIONAL

IS NOT ALWAYS EXPEDIENT

THERE ARE WORTHIER GOALS

THAN TRYING TO MAKE OTHERS

LOVE YOU

A STILLED TONGUE

SILENCES MANY AN ADVERSARY

THE ELEPHANT DOES NOT OBEY

IT AGREES

~ 321 ~

IT IS NOT NECESSARY

TO PLACE YOUR HAND IN FIRE

TO PROVE THAT FIRE BURNS

~ 322 ~

AIR WHAT HAS BEEN MADE PUBLIC

NOT WHAT HAS BEEN MADE PRIVATE

MANY ROADS

ONE DESTINATION

~ 324 ~

CHECK

CHECK AGAIN

CHECK AGAIN

~ 325 ~

IMPORTANT

NOT VITAL

YOU DON'T KNOW THE ENDING

DON'T LIVE LIKE YOU DO

SET

ACT

ACHIEVE

~ 328 ~

LIKE NO OTHER

NO OTHER LIKE

~ 329 ~

GIVEN A CHOICE

MAKE SENSE

BE WORTHY OF PEACE

DON'T COUNT ON MAYBE

SANS DISCIPLINE

CHANCE DECIDES

~ 333 ~

BEHIND EVERY MASK

A FACE

BEHIND EVERY ILLUSION

A REALITY

~ 334 ~

NO MYSTERY

NO SURPRISE

~ 335 ~

DON'T WAIT

FOR WHAT YOU KNOW IS NOT COMING

LEARN THE WAYS OF YOUR FOE

AND BE VICTORIOUS

THINGS DID NOT END WELL

FOR GOLIATH

~ 338 ~

BE AT PEACE

WITH THE WORLDS AROUND YOU

~ 339 ~

FORTUNE

SMILES ON THE RESPONSIBLE

~ 340 ~

REGROUP

THEN RECOUP

IF YOU DON'T HAVE TIME

MAKE TIME

SOMEONE ALWAYS KNOWS

IT MATTERS NOT TO THE FLY

THAT IT PESTERS

STRIVE TO BE EVER ALERT

LIFE IS A GIFT

OPEN YOURS

~ 346 ~

FREE IS ONE WHO IS ABLE TO SING

WHEN IT RAINS

ABANDON WHAT CAUSES YOU GRIEF

~ 348 ~

NEITHER THE KING NOR THE QUEEN

CEDES THE CROWN THOUGHTLESSLY

TRUTH IS NOT PLIANT

~ 350 ~

TIME IS IRRETREVIABLE

USE IT SENSIBLY

~ 351 ~

WHAT AMUSES YOU TODAY

MIGHT ANNOY YOU TOMORROW

THOSE WHO ONLY LOOK OUT FOR

#1

USUALLY END UP STEPPING IN

#2

WHERE YOU LACK MUSCLE

INJECT WIT

WORK SHINES BEST

THROUGH DISCOMFORT

LET TROUBLE FIND PRIDE

WHERE ONCE YOU STOOD

~ 356 ~

A HARD HEAD DOES LITTLE GOOD

FOR A STUBBORN MIND

HELL WILL WAIT

~ 358 ~

IT IS FOLLY TO DESIRE

WHAT YOU KNOW YOU CANNOT HAVE

WEIGH AND MEASURE

INVOLVING ALL

BEING WHO YOU ARE

IS KEY TO LIVING

BE STEADFAST IN ALLIANCE

NOT FOOLISH

~ 362 ~

TRUST LOVE

~ 363 ~

FOR THE GENEROUS

AN OFFER OF PAYMENT IS ENOUGH

IT'S NOT WHAT YOU HEAR

IT'S WHAT YOU HEED

~ 365 ~

THE POSITION OF GOD

HAS ALREADY BEEN FILLED

Contact

email,
wlondea@gmail.com

Twitter,
William E. Londea@WmLondea

ebook available at,

amazon.com ~ barnesandnoble.com

smashwords.com ~ kobobooks.com

dieselbookstore.com ~ itunes.apple.com

THANK YOU!

www.ingramcontent.com/pod-product-compliance
Lightning Source LLC
Chambersburg PA
CBHW020938180426
43194CB00038B/227